THE CALL

LEADER GUIDE

D1570855

THE CALL
THE LIFE AND MESSAGE OF THE APOSTLE PAUL

The Call
978-1-630-88262-4
978-1-630-88263-1 *eBook*

**The Call:
Large Print Edition**
978-1-630-88264-8

The Call: DVD
978-1-630-88267-9

The Call: Leader Guide
978-1-630-88265-5
978-1-630-88266-2 *eBook*

The Call: Youth Study
978-1-630-88268-6
978-1-630-88269-3 *eBook*

**The Call: Children's
Leader Guide**
978-1-630-88270-9

For more information,
visit www.AdamHamilton.org

Also by Adam Hamilton

*24 Hours That Changed
    the World*

*Christianity and World
    Religions*

Christianity's Family Tree

Confronting the Controversies

Enough

Final Words from the Cross

Forgiveness

Leading Beyond the Walls

Love to Stay

Making Sense of the Bible

Not a Silent Night

Revival

*Seeing Gray in a World of
    Black and White*

*Selling Swimsuits
    in the Arctic*

The Journey

The Way

Unleashing the Word

When Christians Get It Wrong

Why?

ADAM HAMILTON

THE
CALL

THE LIFE AND MESSAGE OF
THE APOSTLE PAUL

LEADER GUIDE
by Martha Bettis Gee

Abingdon Press / Nashville

THE CALL:
THE LIFE AND MESSAGE OF THE APOSTLE PAUL

Leader Guide
by Martha Bettis Gee

This book is printed on elemental, chlorine-free paper.

ISBN 978-1-63088-265-5

15 16 17 18 19 20 21 22 23 24—10 9 8 7 6 5 4 3 2 1
MANUFACTURED IN THE UNITED STATES OF AMERICA

CONTENTS

TO THE LEADER

Welcome! In this study, you have the opportunity to help a group of learners as they explore Paul's story, hear his message, and reflect on the meaning of his life and message for their own lives and for our world today. As author Adam Hamilton observes, it could be reasonably argued that no other human, apart from Jesus himself, has had a greater impact on the world than Paul of Tarsus.

It is true that Paul has not been without his critics, both in the first-century church and today. For Hamilton, many of the critiques offered of Paul and his ministry are mitigated by the fact that Paul was a man of his times, for whom the context of ministry was the Greco-Roman world of the first century. Like every Christian from the first century to the twenty-first, his understanding of the gospel was molded by his own faith crises and spiritual experiences. Hamilton believes that Paul's life, when viewed as a whole, reveals a heroic figure who sought to exemplify what it means to follow Jesus Christ faithfully.

Throughout the study, Hamilton suggests that the learner ask the question, "How does this part of Paul's story speak to my life today?" Ultimately, the aim of the study is not simply to teach about Paul, but to help Christians in today's world deepen their faith and answer God's call upon their lives.

Scripture tells us that where two or three are gathered together, we can be assured of the presence of the Holy Spirit, working in and through all those gathered. As you prepare to lead your group, pray for that presence and expect that you will experience it.

This six-session study makes use of the following components:

- the study book *The Call: The Life and Message of the Apostle Paul*, by Adam Hamilton;
- this Leader Guide;
- the video segments that accompany the study.

Participants in the study will also need Bibles, as well as either a paper or electronic means of journaling. If possible, notify those interested in the study in advance of the first session. Make arrangements for them to get copies of the book so they can read the Introduction and Chapter 1.

The Call can become a churchwide program through use of the Youth Study Book and Children's Leader Guide, six-week studies for younger Christians that enable churches and families to study the same material each week on the life of Paul. Preaching and worship can also be included in a churchwide program.

Using This Guide with Your Group

Because no two groups are alike, this guide has been designed to give you flexibility and choice in tailoring the sessions for your group. The session format is listed below. You may choose any or all of the activities, adapting them to meet the schedule and needs of your particular group.

In many cases your session time will be too short to do all the activities. Select ahead of time which activities the group will do, for how long, and in what order. In one or more sessions, use of online video and music selections are suggested. Though these online elements can give participants a multisensory experience, they are not essential to the study.

In each session, you will be presented with a variety of activities from which to choose. Depending on which activities you select, there may be special preparation needed, which will be described in this guide.

Session Format

Planning the Session
   Session Goals
   Biblical Foundation
   Special Preparation
Getting Started
   Opening Activity
   Opening Prayer
Learning Together
   Video Study and Discussion
   Bible and Book Study Discussion
Wrapping Up
   Closing Activities
   Closing Prayer

Helpful Hints

Preparing for the Session

- Pray for the leading of the Holy Spirit as you prepare for the study. Pray for discernment for yourself and for each member of the study group.
- Before each session, familiarize yourself with the content. Read the book chapter again.
- Choose the session elements you will use during the group session, including the specific discussion questions you plan to cover. Be prepared, however, to adjust the session as group members interact and as questions arise. Prepare carefully, but allow space for the Holy Spirit to move in and through the group members and through you as facilitator.
- If you plan to use online clips or images, obtain a video projector. Adults with smartphones can access the clips in that way, but this method is less effective with a group.
- Prepare the group meeting space to enhance the learning process. Ideally, group members should be seated around a table or in a circle so that all can see each other. Movable chairs are best, because the group will often be forming pairs or small groups for discussion.
- Bring a supply of Bibles for those who forget to bring their own. Having a variety of translations is helpful. Adults with smartphones can also find a variety of translations online.
- For most sessions you will also need a chalkboard and chalk, a whiteboard and markers, or an easel with paper and markers.

Shaping the Learning Environment

- Begin and end on time.
- Create a climate of openness, encouraging group members to participate as they feel comfortable. Be on the lookout for signs of discomfort or uncertainty in those who may be silent, and encourage them to express their thoughts and feelings honestly.
- Remember that some people will jump right in with answers and comments, while others need time to process what is being discussed.
- If you notice that some group members seem never to be able to enter the conversation, ask them if they have thoughts to share. Give everyone a chance to talk, but keep the conversation moving. Moderate to prevent a few individuals from doing all the talking.
- Communicate the importance of group discussions and group exercises.
- If no one answers at first during discussions, do not be afraid of silence. Count silently to ten, then say something such as, "Would anyone like to go first?" If no one responds, venture an answer yourself and ask for comments.
- Model openness as you share with the group. Group members will follow your example. If you limit your sharing to a surface level, others will follow suit.
- Encourage multiple answers or responses before moving on.
- Ask, "Why?" or "Why do you believe that?" or "Can you say more about that?" to help continue a discussion and give it greater depth.

- Affirm others' responses with comments such as "Great" or "Thanks" or "Good insight"—especially if it's the first time someone has spoken during the group session.
- Monitor your own contributions. If you are doing most of the talking, back off so that you do not train the group to listen rather than speak up.
- Remember that you do not have all the answers. Your job is to keep the discussion going and encourage participation.

Managing the Session

- Honor the time schedule. If a session is running longer than expected, get consensus from the group before continuing beyond the agreed-upon ending time.
- Involve group members in various aspects of the group session, such as saying prayers or reading Scripture.
- Note that the session guides sometimes call for breaking into smaller groups or pairs. This gives everyone a chance to speak and participate fully. Mix up the groups; don't let the same people pair up for every activity.
- As always in discussions that may involve personal sharing, confidentiality is essential. Group members should never pass along stories that have been shared in the group. Remind the group members at each session: confidentiality is crucial to the success of this study.

1.

CALLED TO
FOLLOW CHRIST

*Paul's Background, Conversion,
and Early Ministry*

*[And Paul said,] "I am a Jew, born in Tarsus in Cilicia . . . a citizen of an
important city. . . circumcised on the eighth day, a member of the people
of Israel, of the tribe of Benjamin, a Hebrew born of Hebrews . . . brought
up in [Jerusalem] at the feet of Gamaliel, educated strictly according
to our ancestral law being zealous for God . . . I advanced in Judaism
beyond many among my people of the same age . . . I persecuted this
Way up to the point of death by binding both men and women and
putting them in prison."*

—Acts 22:3a, 21:39b, Philippians 3:5, Acts 22:3b,
Galatians 1:14a, Acts 22:4

1.

CALLED TO
FOLLOW CHRIST

*Paul's Background, Conversion,
and Early Ministry*

Planning the Session

Session Goals

As a result of conversations and activities connected with this session, group members should:

- begin to form a picture of the man Paul;
- explore how the early experiences and influences in Paul's life were formational;
- begin to make connections between the life and message of Paul and our own life and faith.

Biblical Foundation

[And Paul said,] "I am a Jew, born in Tarsus in Cilicia . . . a citizen of an important city . . . circumcised on the eighth day, a member of the people of Israel, of the tribe of Benjamin, a Hebrew born of Hebrews...brought up in [Jerusalem] at the feet of Gamaliel, educated strictly according to our ancestral law, being zealous for God . . . I advanced in Judaism beyond many among my people of the same age. . . . I persecuted this Way up to the point of death by binding both men and women and putting them in prison."

—Acts 22:3a, 21:39b, Philippians 3:5, Acts 22:3b,
Galatians 1:14a, Acts 22:4

Special Preparation

- Read the entire study book to get a sense of its scope. Pray that the Holy Spirit will be present in and through your preparation and as you lead the first session.
- If possible in advance of the first session, ask those planning to engage in the study to bring either a paper notebook or an electronic means of journaling such as a tablet. Provide writing paper and pens for those who may need them. Also have Bibles for those who do not bring one.
- On a large sheet of paper, print and post the following open-ended prompt:
- When I think of the apostle Paul, what comes to mind is . . . .
- On another large sheet of paper, print and post the following statements from the introduction:

   It could reasonably be argued that no other human, apart from Jesus himself, has had a greater impact on the world than Paul of Tarsus.

   Yet Paul is not without his critics.

- It would be helpful to have available a large map of the area of Paul's missionary journeys to accompany the maps included in the study book.
- From the Internet, download a puzzle template and print off copies of the assembled puzzle for participants. Also have available scissors, envelopes, and glue for participants.
- Gather crayons and colored markers. *(Optional)* Download and print a variety of photographs of nature or other beautiful subject matter.
- This session may include more activities than your group can do in the time you have. Choose from among the activities based on time allotted and the interests and needs of your particular group.

Getting Started

Opening Activity

As participants arrive, welcome them to the study. If group members are not familiar with one another, make nametags available. Provide Bibles for those who did not bring one. Invite the group to respond to the posted open-ended prompt. Jot their responses down on the sheet.

When most participants have arrived, gather together. If they have not already done so, invite group members to read silently the introduction to the study. Call attention to the two posted statements from the Introduction. Invite volunteers to cite some of the evidence the author uses to support his argument about Paul's importance. Then ask the group to name some of Paul's critics and the reasons for their criticism.

Point out that the author is writing out of his own deep appreciation for Paul. Discuss:

- How does the author describe how he views Paul?
- What does he hope will be the result of the book?

Opening Prayer

Holy God, we come together this day eager to make connections between the life and message of Paul and our own life and faith. Guide us as together we seek answers to how Paul's story speaks to our own story, that we may better understand how and to what God is calling us. In the name of Jesus Christ, whom Paul first persecuted and later sought to follow. Amen.

Learning Together

Video Study and Discussion

Briefly introduce Adam Hamilton, the book author and video presenter. Adam Hamilton is senior pastor of The United Methodist Church of the Resurrection in Leawood, Kansas, where he preaches to more than eight thousand per week. Hamilton states his aim is "not simply to teach about Paul, but to help modern-day Christians deepen their own faith and answer God's call upon their lives by studying Paul's life, story, and call." If participants have smartphones, they can learn more about Hamilton and other books he has authored at his website, adamhamilton.org.

Adam Hamilton takes us to key places where the Apostle Paul lived out his ministry. We travel to Tarsus to see where Paul grew up and to Damascus, where as a persecutor of early Christians he met the risen Christ and became a believer.

Fourteen years later, Barnabas took Paul to the church at Syrian Antioch, and Paul's missionary ministry began.

- Paul, in his early training, had "one foot in two worlds" (Greek and Jewish). How do you think this may have affected his life and ministry?
- Paul stood by and may even have approved the stoning of the early church martyr Stephen. How could Paul, as an observant Jew, condone and participate in such actions?
- Paul, blinded physically and spiritually on the road to Damascus, was "right where God needs him to be." What do you think is meant by this?
- How would you have felt if you were Ananias, told by the Holy Spirit to help Paul, the persecutor of Christians? What would you have done?

Bible and Book Study Discussion

Paul's Home and Early Life

Ask a volunteer to read aloud the biblical foundation verses. Invite participants to locate Tarsus on the map in the study book, as well as in the photographs included in the book. If you have a wall map, ask a volunteer to point out Tarsus on that map.

Form two groups. Ask one group to imagine they are writing the copy for a travel agency describing the city of Tarsus—its location, significance (in Paul's time), and any other relevant information from the study book. Invite the other group to create the beginnings of a resumé or curriculum vitae for Paul, focusing on what we know or postulate about Paul's early life. Allow time to work, then ask each group to report. Discuss:

- How do you imagine the location and circumstances of Paul's early life influenced the man he became?

Puzzle Pieces of Life

Ask participants to read silently from the study book under the heading "How God Uses the Puzzle Pieces of Our Lives." Distribute copies of the assembled puzzle template. As the author suggests, invite adults to consider their own background and the question of how God might use the influences and experiences of their growing years. Suggest that they jot these down in their journals, then choose what they consider to be the most significant influences. Invite them to consider the following:

- The author observes that in his experience, the most difficult or painful parts of his past are often the very events that have made good things possible in his adulthood. Would you agree? What are some of the difficult things that have shaped you?

Ask adults to take up the assembled puzzle template and print on each puzzle piece a word or phrase describing a significant event or experience from their early lives. If you downloaded and printed images, encourage adults to choose one image and glue it securely to the reverse side of the assembled puzzle. Alternatively, invite them to use markers or crayons to draw their own images of beauty. If you glued on images, set aside until glue is dry.

Group members will be using their puzzles again at the end of the session.

From Persecutor to Advocate

If they have not already done so, ask the group to read quickly over the information from the heading "Saul the Persecutor" through "The Importance of Ananias." Ask volunteers to read aloud the Scripture references in the study book that sketch out the story of this time period in Paul's life (Acts 7:58-60; 8:1, 3; 9:1-2, 11, 13, 17-18; 26:12-15). Discuss some of the following:

- The author observes that it was Paul's personal ambition, coupled with his unwavering religious conviction, that motivated his persecution of the followers of the Way and specifically his volunteering to oversee Stephen's execution. He suggests that these two motivating factors can be a dangerous combination. Do you agree? Why or why not?
- In what ways or in what circumstances do you struggle with ambition?
- What is a goad? Have you experienced God goading you through the gentle nudgings of someone else? How did you respond?
- Has someone served as your Ananias? Looking back, can you identify a time when you believe God was using you as an Ananias for someone else?

The In-Between Time

Ask the group to scan the study book beginning with the information under the heading "Beginning to Preach" through

"Paul's Sojourn in Arabia and Back in Damascus." Invite volunteers to read the passages in the study book about this time in Paul's life (Acts 9:19b-22; 23; Galatians 1:11-17). Discuss:

- Which other biblical figures spent time in the wilderness? How was their time spent there?
- While we cannot be sure about Paul's sojourn, the author speculates that Paul may have spent the three years working out his theology. What do you think?
- The author suggests that we all need times for silence and solitude for study, prayer, reflection, and listening for God's voice. How and where in your life do you make time for these spiritual practices?

Ask someone to summarize what the study book has to say about the term "the Jews." Encourage group members to keep this information in mind as they continue the study.

Invite the group to quickly read over the information under the heading "Paul and Peter: An Uncomfortable Relationship?" Have volunteers read aloud Galatians 1:18-19 and 2:1-11 and Acts 9:26-27; 28-30. Head a large sheet of paper with the words "Paul" and "Peter." Invite the group to describe each man, and write down the descriptors under the appropriate name. Discuss:

- The author suggests reasons why there may have been tension between Paul and Peter. What is your response to these suggestions? In what ways might the differences between the two men have played into their strained relationship?

- How do both the Gospel accounts and Paul's letters contribute to your understanding of the gospel?

Refer the group to the information under the heading "The In-Between Time." The author tells us that Paul returned to his home, Tarsus, and apparently lived there for some years after his conversion before beginning his ministry. Invite the group to consider the question posed here:

- Are you in the in-between years?

Suggest that while this question applies to young adults trying to discern their vocation, it can also apply to adults in their middle years contemplating a vocational change, either forced on them by a job loss or by choice. Or it could apply to adults entering retirement and struggling with how they might live out their discipleship in their later years.

The Role of Barnabas

Invite someone to find Antioch of Syria on the large map (if available), or have participants locate it on the map in the chapter. Also call attention to the photographs. Point out that the author notes there were at least fourteen cities in Asia Minor and Syria at the time with the name Antioch, two of which were significant in Paul's story.

Ask someone to read aloud Acts 4:36-37, where Barnabas enters the story. Invite another volunteer to read aloud Acts 11:19-26. Discuss:

- How did Barnabas exemplify the meaning of his name?

Wrapping Up

Closing Activities

Learning from Paul's Life

Invite the group to consider what they have learned about Paul's early life and the time spent between his conversion and the beginning of his ministry. Ask:

- What particularly struck you about what you learned? What came as a surprise? What would you like to know more about?

Record these observations on a large sheet of paper and set it aside to add to and consider later in the study.

Ways to Deepen Faith

In this chapter, the author offers several suggestions of practices to deepen the life of faith. Encourage participants during the coming week to try some of his suggestions or one or more of the following:

- **Reflect on the Puzzle Pieces of Life.** Distribute scissors and ask participants to cut apart their puzzles. Give them envelopes in which to store the pieces. Suggest that they reassemble the puzzle at home, reading what they recorded on each piece and reflecting on the following:
  o How has each puzzle piece shaped your life of faith?
  o How might God use each puzzle piece to make something beautiful?

- **Breath Prayer.** The author suggests using a line from Psalm 115:1 as a breath prayer as a means of submitting our ambition to God. "Not to us, O Lord, not to us, but to your name give glory." Another breath prayer, this one to focus our attention on other parts of our lives, might be from the hymn "Amazing Grace": "I once was lost, but now am found" on the inhale; "Was blind, but now I see" on the exhale.

- **Who Is Your Barnabas?** Ask adults to reflect on the two questions that end the chapter: Who is your Barnabas? Whose Barnabas will you be? Suggest that they give thanks to God in prayer for their Barnabas, and pray for discernment as to how they might fill that role for another.

Remind the group to read Chapter 2 before the next session.

"Amazing Grace"

Tell the group the story of the hymn. John Newton became involved in the Atlantic slave trade. In 1748, a violent storm battered his vessel off the coast of Donegal in Ireland so severely that he called out to God for mercy, a moment that marked his spiritual conversion. Newton wrote the first verse of the hymn to mark that experience.

Sing or recite the first verse of the hymn together.

Closing Prayer

Gracious God, we give thanks for the light of your love that illuminates our lives and turns us away from destructive patterns. Grant us insight into how you would have us serve you. In the name of Jesus Christ. Amen.

2.

CALLED TO GO

Paul's First Missionary Journey

Now in the church at Antioch there were prophets and teachers: Barnabas, Simeon who was called Niger, Lucius of Cyrene, Manaen a member of the court of Herod the ruler, and Saul. While they were worshiping the Lord and fasting, the Holy Spirit said, "Set apart for me Barnabas and Saul for the work to which I have called them." Then after fasting and praying they laid their hands on them and sent them off. So, being sent out by the Holy Spirit, they went.

—Acts 13:1-4a

2.

CALLED TO GO

Paul's First Missionary Journey

Planning the Session

Session Goals

As a result of conversations and activities connected with this session, group members should:

- chart Paul's first missionary journey;
- examine the journey's successes and the opposition it encountered;
- be introduced to Paul's theology of sin;
- explore how Paul organized to nurture leadership in the early church;
- continue to make connections between the life and message of Paul and their own lives and faith.

Biblical Foundation

Now in the church at Antioch there were prophets and teachers: Barnabas, Simeon who was called Niger, Lucius of Cyrene, Manaen a member of the court of Herod the ruler, and Saul. While they were worshiping the Lord and fasting, the Holy Spirit said, "Set apart for me Barnabas and Saul for the work to which I have called them." Then after fasting and praying they laid their hands on them and sent them off. So, being sent out by the Holy Spirit, they went....

—Acts 13:1-4a

Special Preparation

- On a large sheet of paper or a board, print and post the following: What is the difference between mission work *to* people and partnering *with* them?

- Recruit a strong reader to read aloud the sermon Paul made at Antioch in Acts 13:16b-41. If you like, ask your reader to use *The Message* or another version in contemporary language, and provide a copy or refer the reader to an online Bible website such as Bible Gateway.

- For the closing prayer, obtain copies of the hymn "Spirit of the Living God" or choose an online version of the hymn and arrange to project it.

- This session may include more activities than your group can do in the time you have. Choose from among the activities based on time allotted and the interests and needs of your particular group.

Getting Started

Opening Activity

As participants arrive, welcome them.

When most participants have arrived, gather together. Ask volunteers to report on what spiritual practice activities they tried since the last session. What insights surfaced as they reflected and prayed?

As a way of reviewing, ask participants to turn to the timeline for Chapter 1. Briefly go over the events in Paul's early life, his conversion, and the time afterward before he began his ministry. Invite someone to read aloud Acts 11:27-30.

Moving on to Chapter 2, point out the posted question: What is the difference between mission work *to* people and partnering *with* them? Invite responses from participants by asking:

- How do you interpret what Paul says in 2 Corinthians 8:13-14 about the importance of striking a "fair balance between your present abundance and their need, so that their abundance may be for your need"?
- What does the author say is God's most common way of answering prayers? How do we make ourselves receptive to God's voice?

Opening Prayer

Help us, Holy God, to listen, pay attention, and seek to hear your continuing call for our ministry. Make us truly receptive to what you may reveal to us in your word today and what we may learn from each other. In the name of Jesus Christ we pray. Amen.

Learning Together

Video Study and Discussion

Paul and Barnabas left on the First Missionary Journey, traveling on sea and land over the Taurus Mountains to cities in Galatia, including Pisidian Antioch, Iconium, Lystra, and Derbe, where he preached to Jews and Gentiles and started some of the first churches in Asia Minor.

- Paul was trained as a tentmaker. How do you think he felt leaving his profession and becoming a missionary?
- Paul traveled for weeks at a time to preach the gospel. Why did he do it? Is it something you would do?
- On arriving in a town, why did Paul usually go first to the synagogue? What are some of the experiences he had at synagogues in Galatia?
- Barnabas's name meant "son of encouragement." What role did he play in Paul's early ministry? Is there someone to whom you can be a Barnabas?

Bible and Book Study Discussion

Hearing God's Call

On the wall map (if available), ask a volunteer to trace Paul and Barnabas's journey from Syrian Antioch to Jerusalem to deliver relief to the Jewish Christians, and back to Antioch. Or ask participants to do so on the map in the study book.

Ask someone to read aloud Acts 13:2-3. Discuss some of the following:

- The author observes that among the times when he is most likely to hear God speaking is when he is in congregational worship. Have you ever experienced times in worship when you felt the Spirit was speaking to you? If so, describe what happened.
- He contends that our role in worship is to prepare ourselves spiritually to hear the Spirit speak—sometimes in spite of, not because of, the music or the preaching. Do you agree? How do you prepare yourself to encounter God in worship?
- Have you ever fasted? If so, was it as a part of a commitment made by a worshiping community, or did you choose to fast as an individual? Describe the experience.
- The author observes that the bulletin at the church he serves does not include the order of worship. What is in the bulletin? Why?

The "First" Missionary Journey

Note the heading of this section in the book. Ask:

- Why did the author place the word *first* in quotation marks?
- If what we call Paul's first missionary journey was in fact not the first, then what set this journey apart from those that came before?
- In addition to Barnabas, who began the journey with Paul? Did that person complete the journey? What happened?

Point out that, beginning with Acts 13:13, Luke shifts from speaking of "Barnabas and Saul" to "Paul and Barnabas." Ask:

- To what does the author attribute this shift?

The author asks readers to consider their own responses to training a mentor who then is promoted to be their boss. Ask:

- If this has happened to you, tell about how you responded, and why.

Hear and Discuss Paul's Sermon

Point out that Paul's usual habit upon entering a town was to go to the synagogue and begin teaching. Invite the group to imagine being among the regular attenders at the synagogue in Pisidian Antioch—Jews and God-fearers—as Paul began to speak. (Remind participants that Pisidian Antioch was different from Syrian Antioch, the city of Paul's home church.) Ask the recruited reader to present Paul's sermon.

On a sheet of paper or a board, print the word *hamartia*, and tell the group that this Greek word literally means to miss the mark. Discuss some of the following:

- Paul uses the word *hamartia* in several different ways. What are they? How do you define sin?
- The author contends that nearly all the problems plaguing humankind have their roots in sin. Would you agree? Why or why not?
- How does the author summarize Paul's teachings?
- In what way does Paul's teaching about salvation have profound implications for Judaism?

Facing Opposition

Invite volunteers to describe briefly the opposition that Paul and Barnabas faced in Pisidian Antioch the following Sabbath.

Remind participants who "the Jews" are in this account, and point out that the Jews who opposed Paul followed him from Antioch to the next towns. Then have someone to read aloud Acts 13:8-20. Ask:

- How might jealousy have fed the opposition Paul encountered on his journey? Where have you encountered jealousy in your faith life, and how did you deal with it? When have you yourself been jealous?
- What does this account have to say about Paul's perseverance?

Explore Nurturing Leaders

Luke tells us that instead of continuing on to Tarsus, when Paul and Barnabas left Derbe they returned to the cities where they had just preached and had encountered opposition. Ask someone to read the excerpt from Titus that is included in the study book (Titus 1:5-9). Referring to that passage as well as to the information in the study book, invite the group to name the positive qualities Paul suggests are needed in elders, and then the negative traits that should be avoided. List both sets of traits on a large sheet of paper or a board. Ask:

- How do these positive and negative traits compare with what we look for when we consider persons for leadership roles in the church? What additional criteria does the church have for leaders?
- What vehicle did Paul use to encourage, mentor, and help the new elders?

Wrapping Up

Closing Activities

Learning from Paul's Life

Call attention to the large sheet of paper on which you recorded the group's thoughts about Paul's early life. Invite the group to consider what they have learned through their consideration of Paul's first missionary journey. Ask:

- What particularly struck you about this first journey? What came as a surprise? What would you like to know more about?

Record these observations on an additional sheet of paper, and set it aside to add to and consider later in the study.

More Ways to Deepen Faith

This chapter suggests more practices that can be used to deepen the life of faith. Some participants may want to continue with prayer practices begun in the last session. Suggest that others may want to consider one of the following:

- **Preparing for and Experiencing the Spirit in Worship.** Remind the group of the question you discussed about how we prepare ourselves to hear the Spirit speaking in worship. Suggest that one way might be to find out in advance of worship what the Scripture readings will be and to read them and reflect on how God may be speaking through them. Encourage participants to try the author's suggestion of taking paper and pencil (or a tablet) to worship in the expectation of receiving a word from God.

- **Explore Fasting.** If participants have never fasted, suggest that they may want to explore this practice further. Fasting traditionally involves abstaining from food, but it often also means abstaining from whatever may be blocking one's ability to attend to God's voice—screen time and social media, for example.
- **Consider Nurture.** Adults who are involved in some way in the leadership of the congregation may want to reflect in the coming week on their own positive and negative traits for leadership. What might they need in order to further nurture their ability to serve God and the church?
- **Perseverance and Faith.** Some may want to reflect further on how Paul's perseverance may inform their faith life. They may want to pray for insight about how to hold strong to what they believe in the face of pressures in the workplace, in the culture at large, or at home.
- **Other.** Invite the group to suggest other ways to strengthen their faith that might arise out of further exploring Paul's life and ministry.

Wherever the Spirit Leads

Remind the group that Paul's travels in this chapter were called Paul's first *missionary* journey because prior to that time he had taken the gospel to familiar territory. Ask the group to close their eyes and become aware of the presence of the Holy Spirit in their midst, as Jesus promised wherever two or three are gathered together.

First, invite them to consider the familiar places where they live out their Christian faith—at home, at church, in the workplace, among friends—and to pray for the Spirit's guidance as they seek to live as disciples in those places and with those people.

Then ask them to invite the Spirit to speak in and through other people and unfamiliar situations and to lead them to respond as disciples in ways they may not have expected before.

Remind the group to read Chapter 3 before the next session.

Closing Prayer

As a closing prayer, sing or recite together the hymn, "Spirit of the Living God."

3.

CALLED TO SUFFER

Paul's Second Missionary Journey (1)

Paul and his companions traveled throughout the regions of Phrygia and Galatia because the Holy Spirit kept them from speaking the word in the province of Asia. When they approached the province of Mysia, they tried to enter the province of Bithynia, but the Spirit of Jesus wouldn't let them. Passing by Mysia, they went down to Troas instead. A vision of a man from Macedonia came to Paul during the night. He stood urging Paul, "Come over to Macedonia and help us!" Immediately after he saw the vision, we prepared to leave for the province of Macedonia, concluding that God had called us to proclaim the good news to them.

—Acts 16:6-10 CEB

3.
CALLED TO SUFFER

Paul's Second Missionary Journey (1)

Planning the Session

Session Goals

As a result of conversations and activities connected with this session, group members should:

- be introduced to the first conflict in the early church, how it was resolved, and what resulted from its resolution;
- explore how Paul's second missionary journey was shaped by the Holy Spirit;
- encounter the stories of the conversions of Lydia and the jailer at Philippi;
- consider the history and theology of baptism;
- continue to make connections between the life and message of Paul and their own lives and faith.

Biblical Foundation

Paul and his companions traveled throughout the regions of Phrygia and Galatia because the Holy Spirit kept them from speaking the word in the province of Asia. When they approached the province of Mysia, they tried to enter the province of Bithynia, but the Spirit of Jesus wouldn't let them. Passing by Mysia, they went down to Troas instead. A vision of a man from Macedonia came to Paul during the night. He stood urging Paul, "Come over to Macedonia and help us!" Immediately after he saw the vision, we prepared to leave for the province of Macedonia, concluding that God had called us to proclaim the good news to them.

—Acts 16:6-10 (CEB)

Special Preparation

- If you decide to do the alternate activity of the fishbowl discussion in the opening, place five chairs in a tight circle in the center of the room.
- One activity calls for participants to write in their journals. Have available writing paper and pens for those who do not bring them.
- For the remembering baptism activity at the end of the session, you will need a pitcher of water and a bowl or basin that is large enough to hold the water but still be passed from person to person.
- This session may include more activities than your group can do in the time you have. Choose from among the activities based on time allotted and the interests and needs of your particular group.

Getting Started

Opening Activity

When most participants have arrived, gather together. Ask volunteers to report on the spiritual practices and prayers in which they engaged since the last session. What insights surfaced as they reflected and prayed?

To review, ask participants to turn to the timeline for Chapter 2. Briefly go over the towns Paul and Barnabas visited on the first missionary journey, as well as their success and the opposition they faced. Remind the group that rather than continuing on to Tarsus, Paul and Silas revisited the towns and cities where they had preached before and then returned to their home church in Syrian Antioch. Get someone to read aloud Acts 14:27-28. Ask:

- Are there conflicts you can name that our congregation is facing or has faced in the past?
- With what conflicts is our denomination or the church at-large presently dealing?

Invite adults to name conflicts that come to mind, without discussing or giving opinions about the conflicts. Then say that in today's session, they will explore the first major conflict that the early church faced and how Christians resolved that conflict, and they will begin to learn about Paul's second missionary journey.

Opening Prayer

Gracious God, we have been promised that where two or three are gathered together, there will your Spirit be also. Through that same Spirit, speak to us today, both through your word in Scripture and through our interactions together. For we ask it in the name of Jesus Christ. Amen.

Learning Together

Video Study and Discussion

Paul and Silas began the Second Missionary Journey, taking the gospel to Europe. In Philippi, Paul met and baptized Lydia, drove evil spirits from a slave girl, and was thrown into prison with Silas. An earthquake freed them, and they converted the jailer before leaving Philippi.

- Why did Paul decide to take the gospel to Europe? Have you ever pushed yourself beyond your comfort zone? What happened?
- Why were Paul and Silas thrown into prison after healing the slave girl? How did they escape, and what did they do during the escape?
- Why were the magistrates afraid when they learned Paul was a Roman citizen? Why do you think Paul decided to challenge the magistrates before leaving town?
- What can we learn about suffering from the example of Paul?

Bible and Book Study Discussion

The Jerusalem Council

Ask the group to quickly review the information under the heading "Division on the Ranks." Then invite a volunteer to give a sentence summarizing the theological debate that sparked the early church's first conflict. Ask more volunteers to add details that further describe what was happening and why. What were the major factions and what were their positions?

Have participants scan the information about the Jerusalem Council. Then ask them to pretend to be reporters covering the council meeting. Have them outline the story in their journals, beginning by creating a headline, then jotting down details of the arguments presented and the major players, then composing a final sentence to give the results of the council. Ask a volunteer to share the story outline.

Alternate activity: Engage in a fishbowl debate. Ask for volunteers to portray Peter, Paul, a "God-fearer," and a member of the council. Have these four characters take four of the chairs you set up earlier, and invite them to have a discussion of the issue. At any point in the discussion, other participants can choose to occupy the fifth chair and join the discussion. After allowing a few minutes for discussion, debrief the activity. Discuss:

- The results of the council were most remarkable. Why?
- What can we learn from that council about how to address conflict in the church?
- Why does the author assert that the council's decisions likely sealed the fate of Christianity as a separate religion from Judaism?

Conflict with a Colleague

Conflict not only emerged in the life of the early church, it surfaced in Paul's own personal life and in his relationship with Barnabas. Invite a volunteer to describe briefly what the conflict was about. Discuss:

- Like all of us, sometimes Paul's greatest strengths could also be his greatest weaknesses. How did Paul's perseverance play into his disagreement with Barnabas?
- What are your strengths? In what ways can they also be weaknesses?
- How did this disagreement affect Paul's second missionary journey? Who accompanied him on this journey?

Paul's Second Journey

Using the material in the study book as well as the map, and a wall map if available, trace together the route of the second journey. Discuss:

- Who joined Paul and Silas at Derbe?

To get a picture of who Timothy was, invite someone to read aloud Acts 16:1-3, 1 Timothy 1:5, and 2 Timothy 3:14-16. Also ask someone to read aloud the footnote in the study book about Timothy. Ask:

- Given the controversy over circumcision, were you surprised to read that Paul had Timothy circumcised? How do you respond to the reasons the author relates in the footnote?

Invite someone to read aloud the biblical foundation verses, Acts 16:6-10. Discuss some of the questions the author poses in the study book:

- Have you ever been prevented from going where you wanted to go and doing what you wanted to do? What were the circumstances, how did you feel, and what were your reactions?

- Was there an occasion when you experienced disappointment, only to have new and amazing opportunities open up for you? Looking back, how do you interpret this experience?
- Have you ever had a vision of your own Macedonia man? If so, to what did you sense you were being called? What did you do?

Ask someone to read aloud Acts 16:10. Note that for the first time, Luke's account uses the word *we* to describe Paul and his traveling companions. Ask:

- What does the word *we* suggest about who might have joined the missionary journey?

Ministry at Philippi

Call the group's attention to the map in the study book that shows Philippi. Form two small groups. Assign to each group one of the following: Acts 16:11-15 and the material in the study book about Lydia's conversion; Acts 16:17-40 and the material about the Philippian jailer. Ask the groups to spend some time exploring the Scripture passages and the author's commentary. They will present the information about their assigned passage to the large group, addressing some of the following:

- a description of the person or persons who were converted;

- anything surprising or unusual about the situation or the people involved;
- the circumstances of the baptisms;
- theological issues raised by the author.

Groups can choose to report in a straightforward way, or they might have one member take the part of the main character or characters for their report.

If the following questions are not addressed in the presentations, discuss some of them in more detail now:

- The author points out times when Paul treated women with dignity and other times when Paul seemed to relegate women to a subordinate role. What explanation does the author give for this apparent contradiction? How do you respond?
- When Paul released the young woman in Acts 16 from her demon, she was then unable to make money for her owners. Often an encounter with the power of Christ will come at some economic cost. Have you ever experienced this? What happened?
- Paul and Silas experienced suffering while in prison in Philippi. How did they respond? What do you make of the fact that Paul did not make known his Roman citizenship until he was released? When have you endured suffering? Do you agree with the author that our faith changes how we face suffering?
- Reflect on what you think it means to speak the "word of God." How do you share your faith?

Wrapping Up

Closing Activities

Learning from Paul's Life

As you have done in the first two sessions, invite the group to consider what they have learned from a consideration of the first significant conflict in the early church and from Paul's second missionary journey. Ask:

- What particularly struck you about these events? What came as a surprise? What would you like to know more about?

Record these observations on an additional sheet of paper and set it aside with the sheets from previous sessions to consider later in the study.

More Ways to Deepen Faith

The stories in this chapter suggest more practices to deepen the life of faith or questions to consider. Some participants may want to continue with prayer practices begun in previous sessions. Suggest that others may want to consider one of the following:

- **Imaging Prayer on Conflict.** Some participants may want to spend the coming week offering a conflict situation to God in prayer. Suggest that they identify either a situation or issue about which the church is in conflict or, more personally, a person with whom they have an unresolved conflict. After centering themselves in prayer, they might extend their hands, palms cupped, imagining holding the situation or the person up to God in prayer. Encourage them to be receptive to what the Spirit may say to them.

- **Who Is Your John Paul or Timothy?** Recall for participants that they considered a person in their life who has served as their Barnabas. Invite them to consider who might be persons they could mentor, as Paul did John Paul and Timothy. Mentoring involves not only offering an example of strength but also of how to deal with one's weaknesses.

- **Other.** Invite the group to suggest other ways to strengthen their faith arising out of what they have learned about Paul's life and ministry.

Explore and Remember Baptism

Invite the group to scan the information in the study book about baptism. Form pairs. Ask one person in each pair to make the case for infant baptism and the other to speak in favor of believer baptism. Then ask one person in each pair to present the case for immersion and the other for "sprinkling" or pouring water. Make these assignments arbitrarily in each pair, regardless of the actual beliefs of each person.

Back in the large group, invite volunteers to tell what they know or have been told about their own baptisms. Some may have been baptized at confirmation or as adults, while others may have been baptized as infants and have no actual memory of it. If there happen to be any adults who have not been baptized, remind the group that the sacrament is just a sign and seal, though a very significant one, of what has already been initiated by God.

Remind the group that in the video they saw the author remembering his own baptism as he lay in the waters of the Gangites River just west of the ruins of Philippi, where Paul baptized Lydia. Invite the group to join in the following ritual to remember their own baptisms.

Form a circle. Pour water from a pitcher into a bowl, raising it high so participants can hear it splashing. Then turn to the person on your right and say, "(Name), remember your baptism and be thankful." That person dips hands in the bowl, then turns to the person on his or her right, passes the bowl, and repeats the same words. Continue around the circle until all have had the opportunity to remember their baptisms. If someone has not been baptized, invite him or her to reflect on God's grace freely extended. Allow for a time of silence.

Remind the group to read Chapter 4 before the next session. If possible, they should also read the first letter to the Thessalonians, as the author encourages readers to do in the chapter.

Closing Prayer

Gracious God, make us ever aware that you pour out your love on us freely. By your Spirit, open our ears and eyes to where you would have us go and what you would have us do, whether in places familiar to us or those unknown. In the name of Jesus Christ the Lord. Amen.

4.

CALLED TO LOVE

Paul's Second Missionary Journey (2)

If I speak in tongues of human beings and of angels but I don't have love, I'm a clanging gong or a clashing cymbal....

Love is patient, love is kind, it isn't jealous, it doesn't brag, it isn't arrogant, it isn't rude, it doesn't seek its own advantage, it isn't irritable, it doesn't keep a record of complaints, it isn't happy with injustice, but it is happy with the truth. Love puts up with all things, trusts in all things, hopes for all things, endures all things....

Now faith, hope, and love remain—these three things—and the greatest of these is love.

—1 Corinthians 13:1, 4-7, 13 CEB

4.

CALLED TO LOVE

Paul's Second Missionary Journey (2)

Planning the Session

Session Goals

As a result of conversations and activities connected with this session, group members should:

- further explore Paul's second missionary journey, his ministry, and the opposition he faced;
- experience Paul's speech in Athens and explore its theology;
- explore parallels between first-century Corinth and twenty-first-century America;
- expand understandings of life and ministry in the early church through an exploration of the first letter to the Corinthians;

- continue to make connections between the life and message of Paul and their own lives and faith.

Biblical Foundation

If I speak in tongues of human beings and of angels but I don't have love, I'm a clanging gong or a clashing cymbal. If I have the gift of prophecy and I know all the mysteries and everything else, and if I have such complete faith that I can move mountains but I don't have love, I'm nothing. If I give away everything that I have and hand over my own body to feel good about what I've done but I don't have love, I receive no benefit whatsoever.

Love is patient, love is kind, it isn't jealous, it doesn't brag, it isn't arrogant, it isn't rude, it doesn't seek its own advantage, it isn't irritable, it doesn't keep a record of complaints, it isn't happy with injustice, but it is happy with the truth. Love puts up with all things, trusts in all things, hopes for all things, endures all things.

Love never fails.... Now faith, hope, and love remain—these three things—and the greatest of these is love.

—1 Corinthians 13 (CEB)

Special Preparation

- As you did in Session 2, recruit a strong reader to read aloud Paul's speech in Athens in Acts 17:22-31. Ask your reader to use the excerpt in the study book, or you may want to use *The Message* or another version in contemporary language.
- On a large sheet of paper or a board, draw a Venn diagram—two large circles that overlap with an intersecting area. Label one circle "First-Century Corinth" and the other "Twenty-First-Century America."

- Provide writing paper and pens for participants who did not bring a journal or tablet.
- This session may include more activities than your group can do in the time you have. Choose from among the activities based on time allotted and the interests and needs of your particular group.

Getting Started

Opening Activity

As participants arrive, welcome them and gather together. Ask volunteers to report on the spiritual practices and prayers in which they engaged since the last session. What insights surfaced as they reflected and prayed? In what ways did they sense the presence and guidance of the Holy Spirit?

To review, ask participants to turn to the maps in Chapter 3 for the places Paul and his companions visited at the beginning of his second missionary journey. Invite volunteers to review what happened in Philippi using the map and timeline.

Invite the group to join in an imaginative visualization of the trip Paul and his colleagues took from Philippi to Thessalonica. Ask them to close their eyes and settle into a comfortable position, then breathe in and out deeply. Say:

> Imagine you are walking with Paul along the Via Egnatia. On your back you are carrying tent, scrolls, clothing, and supplies for the journey. For the past two days you have been trudging over hilly terrain, passing down into valleys and then climbing back up the hills. You have just passed through the town

of Amphipolis. It will take you two more days to reach Apollonia, and after another two days you will finally come to Thessalonica. Your back is aching from carrying the weight of all the things you need for the trek. Your legs are tired, but they are gradually getting stronger as you walk along.

What are your thoughts as you walk? As you anticipate arriving at Thessalonica, what are you hopes for your ministry there? What are your fears?

Tell the group that in this session, they will further explore Paul's second missionary journey, focusing on what happened in Thessalonica, Beroea, Athens, and Corinth.

Opening Prayer

Loving God, we yearn to encounter you in your Word. Make us aware of your presence as we seek to make your story our story. In the name of Jesus Christ we pray. Amen.

Learning Together

Video Study and Discussion

Paul and Silas completed the Second Missionary Journey, traveling to Thessalonica, Berea, and on to Athens, where Paul reasoned with the Athenians at the Areopagus. At the important city of Corinth he countered immorality at the pagan temples with moving words about God's love.

- What approach did Paul take when he preached to the Athenians? Why? What does it teach us about sharing our faith with diverse groups?
- What were some of the issues that Paul preached about in Corinth? Why?
- What kind of city was Corinth? Why was sexual immorality more common there, and how did Paul try to counter it?
- What does Adam Hamilton say we can learn about political disagreements by observing the Corinthians and what Paul told them?

Bible and Book Study Discussion

In Thessalonica and Beroea

Invite a volunteer to read the passage included in the study book, Acts 17:2-4. Point out that Paul's success in preaching at the synagogue in Thessalonica again kindled opposition. Ask:

- What form did Paul's opposition take? What was the result?
- The study book tells us that those opposing Paul and his colleagues accused them of "turning the world upside down." Do you think that accusation can still be made of believers today? Why or why not?
- What does the excerpt in the study book from the first letter to the Thessalonians tell you about Paul's ministry there?

Ask the group to read silently the excerpt about Paul's ministry in Beroea. Note that the same people causing trouble in Thessalonica followed Paul to cause problems in Beroea. Paul left Silas and Timothy in Beroea, urging them to come as soon as they could, and he journeyed to Athens along with some of the new Beroean believers.

In Athens

Ask the group to recall the scenes from Athens from the video segment, and to examine the photos in the study book and read the author's commentary about the city.

Invite the group to imagine themselves to be Athenian intellectuals and philosophers gathered in the marketplace, curious to hear what Paul has to say about this new religion. Give them a few minutes to read in the book the author's commentary on Paul's speech in order to get in character, then set the stage by reading aloud Acts 17:16-22a. Then have your recruited reader deliver Paul's speech. Ask the philosophers and intellectuals to discuss in character:

- What did you think about what Paul had to say about this unknown god?
- Did you notice that he quoted two of our poets? How did he apply those quotes to the god he was talking about?
- What was his argument about not worshiping things made by human hands? Did you agree or disagree? Why?
- What other thoughts do you have about his speech? Do you think you would be willing to hear more?

Ask participants to step out of character and debrief. Discuss:

- Few came to faith under Paul's leadership in Athens, but those few laid the foundations for a church that impacted millions. The author notes that in our churches, numbers are one indicator of success, but they are not the only measure or even the best. How do you define "success" in the church?

- Other than large increases in membership numbers, what other indicators or metrics can you name that might enable us to measure the kind of success you have described?

In Corinth

Ask the group to recall the scenes in Corinth from the video segment and to examine the photos in the study book and read the author's commentary about the city. Invite volunteers to name significant facts about the city that made it a strategic location for commerce. Ask:

- Whom did Paul encounter first in Corinth, and why were those two people there?
- What happened when Paul preached and taught in the synagogue in Corinth? What did he do in response?

Based on what the author tells us in the study book, invite the group to make a comparison between first-century Corinth and twenty-first-century America. First ask them to name things that describe Corinth only—that don't specifically describe life in our context—and to print those things in the appropriate circle in the prepared Venn diagram. Then ask them to name things that describe our cultural context, not Corinth's, and list those in the appropriate circle. Then ask for aspects of life that our context shares with Corinth, and print those in the intersection of the two circles. Discuss:

- Paul devotes more verses to the subject of sexual immorality in 1 Corinthians than in any other letter. What features in Corinthian life might help to explain this?
- To your knowledge, has your pastor addressed issues related to sexual morality in a sermon? If so, how did you respond? If not, how comfortable would you be if your pastor did so?

Examining Letters to the Corinthians

In the four years after Paul visited Corinth, he wrote four letters to the Corinthians, and the book of 1 Corinthians is one of those four.

In 1 Corinthians, and to a lesser degree in 2 Corinthians, we get a window into the issues the Corinthian church was facing. Ask the group to refer to the study book and then to name issues that Paul was addressing in 1 Corinthians. Invite a volunteer to read aloud 1 Corinthians 7:1. Suggest that participants make a list of questions about the life of faith that they would ask Paul if they had the opportunity.

After allowing a few minutes for adults to formulate their lists, ask someone to read a list aloud, and print the questions on a large sheet of paper or a board. Have other volunteers read their lists, adding any questions that are not already included. Continue to add to the list until everyone's questions are included. Ask:

- Given that it is not possible to ask Paul to address our questions, to whom would you direct this list of questions?

If you like, send the list to the person or persons the group identifies. *Alternative:* Include the list in a letter addressed to another congregation, including a salutation ("First Church of Anytown, to the church of _____. Grace to you and peace...") and a conclusion ("The grace of our Lord Jesus Christ be with you").

Wrapping Up

Closing Activities

Learning from Paul's Life

Invite the group to consider what they have learned from a further exploration of Paul's second missionary journey, particularly from his ministry in Thessalonica, Beroea, Athens, and Corinth. Ask:

- What particularly struck you about what you learned? What came as a surprise? What would you like to know more about?

Record these observations on an additional sheet of paper and set it aside with the sheets from previous sessions to consider later in the study.

More Ways to Deepen Faith

Some participants may want to continue with prayer practices begun in the last session. Suggest that others may want to consider one of the following:

- **Walking Prayer.** The author helps us to visualize Paul's journeys by giving us a glimpse of landmarks and terrain and helping us understand the distances Paul and his colleagues had to walk. Remind the group of the imaginative visualization exercise at the beginning of the session. Encourage them to try engaging in walking prayer during the coming week. Suggest that they choose a route for walking, and as they begin, try centering themselves to be receptive to God's spirit. Remind them that Paul and his friends had to carry tents, clothing, and supplies as they walked from town to town. Ask the group to reflect on the following:

o What are the attitudes, ideas, and assumptions I carry with me as I seek to answer God's call?

o Which ones are necessary for equipping me as a disciple?

o Which ones are weighing me down and making my faith journey more difficult?

- **E-mail Conversation.** Participants may want to engage in online conversations among themselves on one or more of the questions they identified during the session about the Christian life. The conversation might be among just participants, or they may want to invite friends in other congregations to join the dialogue.
- **Other.** Invite participants to suggest other possibilities for spiritual practices that may have occurred to them during the session.

A Reflection on 1 Corinthians 13

Remind the group that a possible test of one's spiritual life can be made by inserting one's own name in place of the word *love* as this familiar passage is read aloud. Read aloud the first part of the passage yourself (vv. 1-3). Then invite participants to join you reading verses 4-7 in unison, with each person inserting his or her own name. Conclude by reading verse 8a and verse 13. Allow for a period of silence for participants' individual reflections.

Closing Prayer

Loving God, guide us as we seek to emulate the most profound example of love made incarnate, your Son, Jesus Christ. Make us aware of your presence with us, guiding us by your Spirit as we continue our journey as followers of the Way. In the name of the One who came to show us what your love is like, your Son, Jesus Christ. Amen.

5.

CALLED TO GIVE

Paul's Third Missionary Journey

After some time there he left and traveled from place to place in the region of Galatia and the district of Phrygia, strengthening all the disciples.... [then] Paul took a route through the interior [of Asia Minor] and came to Ephesus.

—Acts 18:23; 19:1 CEB

5.

CALLED TO GIVE

Paul's Third Missionary Journey

Planning the Session

Session Goals

As a result of conversations and activities connected with this session, group members should:

- discover Paul's third missionary journey and his ministry in Ephesus;
- explore the power and influence of the Holy Spirit;
- examine the economic impact of the gospel in Paul's time and the potential impact today;
- make further connections between the life and message of Paul and our own lives and faith.

Biblical Foundation

Now concerning the collection for the saints: you should follow the directions I gave to the churches of Galatia. On the first day of every week, each of you is to put aside and save whatever extra you earn, so that collections need not be taken when I come. And when I arrive, I will send any whom you approve with letters to take your gift to Jerusalem.

—1 Corinthians 16:1-3

Special Preparation

- From your pastor or a member of the church's governing board, obtain copies (if available) of your congregation's annual budget.

- Obtain sheets of drawing paper and pens, as well as lengths of string or yarn for tying up the scrolls that are suggested in the activity of exploring incantation scrolls.

- Recruit a strong reader to deliver Paul's words to the elders in Ephesus in Acts 21:18b-35. If you like, the reader can use *The Message* or another version in contemporary language.

- For the closing activity, get some scented oil, or simply some vegetable oil, and a shallow bowl.

- This session may include more activities than your group can complete in the time you have. Choose from among the activities based on the time allotted to you and the interests and needs of your particular group.

Getting Started

Opening Activity

Welcome the participants. When most of them have arrived, gather together. Ask volunteers to report on the spiritual practices and prayers in which they engaged since the last session. What insights surfaced as they reflected and prayed? In what ways did they sense the presence and guidance of the Holy Spirit?

Form pairs. Distribute copies of your congregation's annual budget to each pair. Ask pairs to take a few moments to get familiar with the budget, noting roughly what percentage of the annual income goes to benevolences and mission and what percentage stays in the local congregation. In the large group, ask volunteers to report what they found. Ask:

- What does our budget reveal about where our priorities are?
- How do our line items reflect our commitment to further the ministry of the larger church?

Tell the group that in this session they will discover how and why Paul encouraged the churches he visited to set aside money for an offering for the mother church in Jerusalem.

Opening Prayer

Gracious God, we know that all good gifts come from you. As we follow in Paul's footsteps today, make us ever more aware of your generous love. Open your Word to us, that we may open our hearts and minds and be stirred to seek your will. In the name of Jesus Christ. Amen.

Learning Together

Video Study and Discussion

Paul felt called to set out on a Third Missionary Journey, first revisiting churches he had founded and then returning to the wealthy city of Ephesus, where he stayed for over two years, boldly proclaiming Christ. His preaching hurt sales of idols, and he was hustled out of town by local Christians to avoid a confrontation with angry merchants.

- Why did Paul find it important to revisit churches he had founded? Why did he write them letters? What do these activities say about his ministry?
- Paul's preaching hurt local businesses. Why did Paul do it? How did they respond?
- How might the activities of you or your church affect the economics of the surrounding community? What can we learn from Paul about how to respond?

Bible and Book Study Discussion

To review, ask the group to scan the portion of Paul's second missionary journey described in the last session, referring to the map and timeline in Chapter 4 and focusing on what happened in Thessalonica, Beroea, Athens, and Corinth. In this session, the group will explore Paul's third missionary journey, focusing on what happened in Ephesus.

Invite the group to turn to the map showing the portion of Paul's next journey from Syrian Antioch to Ephesus and to review what the study book says about the route the author suggests Paul may have taken. Ask adults with smartphones to use a map application to determine a city six hundred miles from your location. Invite the group to imagine walking that distance. Discuss:

- Paul traveled overland from Syrian Antioch to Ephesus, a journey he could have made much more quickly by sea. Why did Paul travel by land?

Invite the group to review the material in Chapter 5 describing Ephesus and to recall what they saw and heard in the video segment. Ask someone to name a relevant detail about the city that particularly struck them, and ask other volunteers to add other facts until a picture of the city emerges.

The Influence and Power of Holy Spirit

Note that Luke places a strong emphasis on the Holy Spirit in both his Gospel and in Acts. Invite a volunteer to read aloud Acts 19:1-7. Discuss:

- The author comments that many Christians today might echo the disciples Paul encountered in Ephesus in saying, "We've not even heard that there is a Holy Spirit." He suggests that not having allowed the Spirit to influence them or exert power in their lives may be one reason that some have an anemic faith. How do you respond? Would you agree or disagree?

Recall that in the opening activity, participants were asked in what ways they had sensed the presence and guidance of the Holy Spirit in the past week. Ask one or two volunteers to describe what the study book tells us Paul has to say about the various ways the Spirit works in the lives of believers. Invite the group to reflect without responding out loud on how they have experienced the Spirit's presence and power. If, like the disciples in Ephesus, this has not been their experience, encourage them to consider why, and how they might be more open to the Spirit.

Ask a volunteer to continue reading Acts 19:8-10. Though we know little of what Paul was doing in Ephesus, it appears he was preaching and teaching. Ask:

- What else does the author suggest Paul was doing to spread the gospel?
- In what ways were Paul's activities similar to what in later times might have been functions of a bishop?

Explore Healing and Exorcism

Form pairs. In each pair, ask one person to discuss what they learned in the book about healing and exorcism in the first century, and ask the other person to discuss possible explanations of healings in biblical times and in our time. In the large group, invite comments or questions that may have arisen in their pairs. Discuss:

- The author suggests that in some cases, healings may be more about the individual's faith than about anything medical. What does he mean? Would you agree or disagree? What other factors do you think might be important in these healings?

Continue by asking volunteers to describe how the incantation scrolls that were sold in Ephesus were meant to work. The author suggests that we may have our own "scrolls"—things in which we have previously put our trust and made our source of hope and security. Ask:

- Are there things you rely on in your life that you need to rid yourself of?
- Are there things that are a distraction, or things that are simply not in keeping with your desire to follow Jesus Christ?

Distribute sheets of paper and pens to participants. Invite participants to consider the questions and identify something in their lives that serves as a distraction from living the Christian life or perceiving the power of the Holy Spirit. Invite each of them to print that distraction on the sheet of paper, roll it up, and tie it with the string or yarn. Set the scrolls aside until the closing activity.

Examining the Economic Impact of the Gospel

Remind the group that in Chapter 3 they explored the account of the slave girl's exorcism, which resulted in economic loss for her owners. Ask a volunteer to read aloud the excerpt from Acts in the study book (Acts 19:23-27). Is the gospel having any kind of economic impact on your community? Discuss some of the following:

- What happened in Ephesus as a result of Paul's teachings about the "gods" that had been made by human hands?

- What are ways in which the gospel, working in the hearts of a significant number of people in our community, might impact our economy?
- Are there spending habits that might change as people commit their lives to Christ? If so, what specific examples can you cite?
- Can you name any moral stands in our community that Christians might take that would have a negative impact on someone's economic gain? If so, what might be the results?

The Offering for the Jerusalem Church

Invite the group to read silently 2 Corinthians 8, Paul's encouragement to the Corinthians to be generous in their offering for the Jerusalem church. Then ask volunteers to read 2 Corinthians 9, round-robin style, taking turns reading a verse or two aloud. Discuss:

- There was a sense of urgency in Paul's words about the offering. Why does the author suggest that it was personal for Paul?

Remind the group that in Chapter 4 they learned of the conflicts that developed in the church at Corinth. Review the four letters that Paul is believed to have written to that church. (These letters were, in order, a lost letter believed to have preceded 1 Corinthians, then 1 Corinthians, then 2 Corinthians 10–13, and finally 2 Corinthians 1–9.) After visiting the Macedonian churches, Paul returned to Corinth, where he stayed for three months. Invite participants to trace

Paul's steps upon leaving Corinth on the wall map (if available) and on the map in the study book.

Set the context for Paul's speech when he arrived in Ephesus:

> Imagine you are the elders in the church at Ephesus, where Paul is arriving to make a final visit before departing for Jerusalem. You have a long personal history with Paul, and now he has asked to meet with you.

Then have your recruited reader deliver Paul's speech. Following the speech, discuss:

- What are your emotions on hearing that Paul is determined to go to Jerusalem, at his own peril?

Wrapping Up

Closing Activities

Learning from Paul's Life

Invite the group to consider what they have learned from this exploration of Paul's third missionary journey. Ask:

- What about the journey particularly struck you? What came as a surprise? What would you like to know more about?

Record these observations on an additional sheet of paper, and set it aside with the sheets from previous sessions to consider in the final session of the study.

More Ways to Deepen Faith

Some participants may want to continue with prayer practices begun in the last session. Suggest that other participants may want to consider one of the following:

- **Pray for Healing.** Regardless of their particular understanding of healing in biblical times and in the early church, participants may want to approach healing with the understanding that it is a part of shalom, which is an all-embracing peace and wholeness that God intends for all of creation. In this vision of healing, we embrace our embodied selves that cannot be separated into physical, emotional, and psychological components. Participants may wish to offer prayers of intercession for God's created order and the social order, or more specifically for a broken relationship or chronic illness.
- **Transforming Our Spending.** Participants who identified a particular spending habit—or an obsession with acquiring stuff—might make a specific commitment to pray for discernment about how to transform that habit.
- **Commit to a "Jerusalem Offering."** Participants may decide to examine their stewardship commitment, perhaps seeking discernment by reading 2 Corinthians 8 and 9 as a part of their devotion time. To what specific mission endeavors might they increase their giving, thereby furthering the work of the church?
- **Burn the Scrolls of Incantation (Security).** Suggest that participants take home the scrolls they created and burn them as a sign of letting go of false sources of security.

- **Other.** Invite participants to suggest other possibilities for spiritual practices that may have occurred to them during the session.

Remind participants to look at Chapter 6 in the coming week. In that chapter, the author encourages us to read the entire story of Paul's arrest in Acts 21:27–22:29. Ask participants to do so before the final session.

Anointing and Laying on of Hands

As part of confirmation and baptism, the author's congregation practices laying on of hands and anointing with oil as a sign of the Spirit's presence and power. In some congregations, both practices are also used in services of healing and wholeness.

Invite the group to form a circle. Tell the group they have an opportunity to be anointed and to anoint one another. Tell participants that if they choose, they can opt out by bowing their heads in a moment of silent prayer when their turn comes.

Turn to the person on your right and dipping your thumb in the bowl of oil, make the sign of the cross on his or her forehead with these words or something similar: "(Name,) you have been sealed by the Holy Spirit and marked as Christ's own forever." That person then takes the bowl and repeats the act with the next person until all have had the opportunity to be anointed.

Allow for a time of silence. If you like, invite the group to turn so they are facing the back of the next person, and lay their hands on that person's shoulders as you pray the following:

Closing Prayer

Holy God, uphold us by your Spirit. Daily increase in us the gifts of your Spirit and the sense of the Spirit's power in our lives. In the name of Jesus Christ. Amen.

6.
CALLED TO BE FAITHFUL

Paul's Death and Legacy

We and the local believers urged Paul not to go up to Jerusalem. Paul replied, "Why are you doing this? Why are you weeping and breaking my heart? I'm ready not only to be arrested but even to die in Jerusalem for the sake of the name of the Lord Jesus."

—Acts 21:12-13 CEB

6.
CALLED TO BE FAITHFUL

Paul's Death and Legacy

Planning the Session

Session Goals

As a result of conversations and activities connected with this session, group members should:

- explore Paul's understanding of the Law and the new covenant;
- trace Paul's journey to Rome and identify what events took place in the course of the trip;
- examine Paul's witnessing about his faith and ponder the power of personal testimony;
- walk along with Paul on the final journey to his death;
- affirm that, like Paul, we are called to follow Jesus.

Biblical Foundation

We and the local believers urged Paul not to go up to Jerusalem. Paul replied, "Why are you doing this? Why are you weeping and breaking my heart? I'm ready not only to be arrested but even to die in Jerusalem for the sake of the name of the Lord Jesus."

—Acts 21:12-13 (CEB)

Special Preparation

- On a large sheet of paper or a board, post the following two journaling prompts:

  o In following Jesus as a disciple, I have felt the call to make the following decisions or take the following actions: _____. Those decisions or actions resulted in the following hardship or suffering: _____.

  o In following Jesus as a disciple, I have never felt the call to make decisions or take actions that resulted in hardship or suffering, or I was faced with a decision or action that I chose not to take. I believe I have never taken such action because_____.

- Recruit a strong reader to deliver Paul's testimony before King Agrippa, included in the chapter.
- If you decide to do the stations activity, "Walking on Paul's Final Journey," post the following signs at intervals around your space:
  o Mamertine Prison: Imprisonment (2 Timothy 4:6-8)
  o St. Mary of the Stairway to Heaven: Holding Cell (Philippians 1:20-24)

  o Church of St. Paul at the Three Fountains: Execution
   (2 Corinthians 4:16-17)
  o Basilica of St. Paul Outside the Walls: Burial
   (Romans 8:31, 35-38)

- Also print and post the following:

  o How and when did you become a Christian?
  o What led you to become a Christian?
  o How have you experienced God working in your life?
  o How has being a Christian positively changed your
   life?

- Post the sheets of paper on which you recorded participants' comments and questions at the end of the previous five sessions.
- Decide if you will use one of the suggested hymns for the closing.
- This session may include more activities than your group can do in the time you have.

Choose from among the activities based on time allotted and the interests and needs of your particular group.

Getting Started

Opening Activity

Welcome participants. When most have arrived, gather together. Ask volunteers to report on the spiritual practices and prayers in which they engaged since the last session. What was their experience in praying for healing? In what ways did they feel the nudging of the Spirit as they examined their spending habits? What other insights surfaced?

Invite participants to reflect on the two posted journaling prompts ("In following Jesus as a disciple..."), then determine which of the two reflects their experience as Christians and record responses in their journals. After allowing a few minutes for them to write, ask volunteers to report on their responses. There are likely those in the group who cannot recall being faced with making a decision or taking an action because of their faith that posed a potential risk to their professional life, to friendships, or to some type of success. If so, ask them to consider:

- Am I following Jesus in ways that challenge me to live more fully as a disciple? If not, why not?

Ask someone to read aloud the passage from 2 Corinthians included in the study book, where Paul offers a litany of the sufferings he had endured in the name of Jesus Christ. Tell the group that in this last session, they will discover how Paul literally put his life on the line for his faith.

Opening Prayer

Holy God, make us receptive to what you would have us hear in your Word today. Stir us to respond to the challenge of following Jesus, even at personal cost to ourselves. In the name of your Son, our Lord Jesus Christ. Amen.

Learning Together

Video Study and Discussion

After leaving Ephesus, Paul traveled to Caeserea, where he was arrested for violating temple rules and was sent to Rome to be tried. After a harrowing trip there, he was held under house arrest for two years, teaching and bringing people to Christ. We learn two traditions about Paul's final years, both ending in his execution at the Mamertine Prison in Rome. We reflect on what Paul's life and death mean for us today.

- How did Paul handle his imprisonment in Rome? What can we learn from it?
- How do you respond to the on-site visits and lessons we've experienced in this series? What do you believe about the sites, and what don't you believe? Why?
- What is the most surprising thing you learned in this study of Paul? the most disappointing? the most moving?
- What are the two or three most important things you will take away from this study? What affect might they have on your actions?

Bible and Book Study Discussion

Paul's Reception in Jerusalem

Call participants' attention to the portion of the book describing Paul's reception by the elders in Jerusalem. Discuss:

- According to the elders, what impression has Paul made on Jewish believers in Jerusalem?

Ask someone to read aloud Acts 21:20-22 (included in Chapter 6). Ask:

- What is interesting about this statement, according to the author?

Form two smaller groups. Ask one group to read and discuss the information in the chapter about Paul's approach to the Law, and the other to read and discuss the information about the new covenant. After allowing a few minutes for groups to work, ask each group to briefly summarize for the other what they learned. Then discuss:

- What is the relationship between the Law and the new covenant?

Ask a volunteer to describe what the elders wanted Paul to do in order to counter his negative image with Jewish Christians, and what happened as a result. Then ask:

- The author describes one of the challenges of religious belief. What is it? What can be one negative result of deeply held passionate convictions?
- The author names two examples of misplaced religious passion. Can you cite other contemporary examples of followers of a faith who unwittingly do the exact opposite of what their faith teaches?

Testimony Before King Agrippa

Point out that following the riot in Jerusalem, Paul was brought before the Sanhedrin, where his testimony again caused an uproar from which the Roman soldiers had to rescue him. Following the discovery of a plot against his life by Jewish leaders, Paul was transferred to Caesarea by the Sea.

Before hearing Paul's testimony before King Agrippa, ask volunteers to give a brief description of the historical context of Acts as included in the study book. Recruit two volunteers, one to take the part of Festus and the other Agrippa. Refer the group to the excerpt from Acts included in the study book, and have your recruited reader read Paul's part, while the volunteers contribute a line each. Discuss:

- What is your response to Paul's testimony?
- What was King Agrippa's verdict? Why does the author suggest Luke included his statement?

Paul's Journey to Rome

Invite the group to locate on the timeline the likely years of Paul's journey to Rome, after two years in Caesarea. Ask a volunteer to read aloud the footnote about Luke's use of the first person plural here. Ask:

- What does the author suggest was the primary intent of Luke's account of Paul's journey?
- Many scholars have noted parallels between Luke's account and Homer's account of the journeys of Odysseus. What reason does the author suggest for this apparent parallel?

Ask participants to read silently the account of Paul's journey to Rome in Acts 27 and 28. Together, list in order the events that happened. When the list is complete, take each event in order and locate on the map in the study book (and on the wall map, if available) where each event took place, tracing Paul's journey to Rome. Point out that nonbelievers consistently showed kindness to Paul. Invite volunteers to read aloud Romans 1:20 and Romans 2:13-16 (the latter included in the study book). Discuss:

- What do these passages have to say about Gentiles who do not know Christ?
- How do you respond to the author's take on eternal fate of people who are not Christians? Do you agree or disagree? Why?

Life in Rome

Invite participants to scan the content on Rome in the study book and the photos of locations in Rome that are associated with Paul, as well as what they noted in the video segment about Rome. Discuss:

- Paul had never been to Rome. What does the author tell us about the churches there?
- As was his custom, Paul first met with the leaders of the Jewish community. What was the outcome of his meeting with those leaders?

Invite a volunteer to read aloud Acts 28:30-31. Discuss:

- The author tells us that scholars have been perplexed by this ending. What two reasons does he give?

Ask participants to refer to the map of Paul's "fourth" missionary journey. Ask:

- What evidence supports Paul's having made a fourth missionary journey? What calls such a journey into question?

Walking on Paul's Final Journey

Tell the group that while Scripture does not record the details or circumstances of Paul's death, tradition does offer some clues. Say that they will take a journey around the classroom and in their imaginations, aided by photos and information in the study book and by what they remember about locations in Rome from the video segment. (See Special Preparation at beginning of this session.)

To set the context, ask participants to read silently the excerpt from the Roman historian Tacitus about the fire that consumed the city during Nero's reign. Invite them to go to the first station you set up ahead of time, bringing their study books with them. At this station, ask them to offer observations about the place they have gleaned from the study book or video. Ask someone to read aloud Philippians 1:20-24. Continue in the same way through the other three stations you have set up, eliciting observations and insights and reading the suggested Scripture passage at each location.

Wrapping Up

Closing Activities

Experiencing the Power of Testimony

Remind participants that over the course of the study they have explored instances when Paul made a personal testimony, often to hostile or skeptical audiences. Call attention to the four questions you posted before class ("How and when did you become a Christian? What led you to become a Christian? How have you experienced God working in your life? How has being a Christian positively changed your life?) and invite participants to take a few minutes to jot down responses in their journals. Encourage them to reflect carefully, avoiding pat answers. Then ask them to form pairs and discuss their responses with a partner.

Back in the large group, invite volunteers to share any insights or observations. Point out that for many Christians who were raised in the church, there may not have been a time when they did not consider themselves Christian, while for other Christians, faith is a new experience. In either case, ask participants to consider who and what has nurtured them over the years to a more mature faith.

Encourage participants to continue pondering the posted questions and to consider how they might better testify to their own personal story of faith.

Reviewing Questions and Insights

Together with the group, review the sheets on which you recorded for each session what particularly struck participants, what came as a surprise, and what they would like to know more about. Ask:

- What questions have now been answered?
- What on these lists are unanswered questions or areas about which you would still like to know more?
- What other insights have you had as a result of this study?

Encourage the group to continue learning about Paul by reading more deeply in the book of Acts, in Paul's letters, and in the study book's list of resources "For Further Reading."

Responding to the Call

Call the group's attention to the information under the final heading at the conclusion of the chapter. Revisit the author's aim in writing this study—in part, for participants to study the life and faith of the Apostle Paul, but also, inspired by his life, to hear God's call and respond as Paul did.

Have a volunteer summarize the author's story of Isabelle. Invite the group to name other contemporary examples of people who have responded to God's call.

Ask the group to form a circle. Read aloud the following from the study book:

> Your call may not be as dramatic as the Apostle Paul's. It may be not be as noble as Isabelle's. But you have been called and continue to be called by Christ. You're called to follow him daily in your life. You're called to be an instrument of his love and grace. You're called to live, give, and serve. As you answer that call, you will find that your own life and the world are changed forever.

Invite participants to ponder the question with which the study closes:

- What won't happen if you don't do what God has called you to do?

Sing or recite a hymn of consecration, such as "Take My Life and Let It Be," "Open My Eyes, That I May See," or "The Summons."

Closing Prayer

Like Paul, O God, we sometimes are blind to your call. Stubbornly we pursue what we want to do, ignoring your will for our lives. Open our eyes to your holy presence, our ears to your call, and our hearts to the movement of your Spirit. We ask it in the name of Jesus Christ our Lord. Amen.